LIFESTYLE POETRY FROM THE
INNER CITY

ANN M. JONES-CHEATHAM

© 2017 Divine Works Publishing
ALL RIGHTS RESERVED

Ann M. Jones-Cheatham
LIFESTYLE POETRY FROM THE INNER CITY
All rights reserved. No part of this publication may be reproduced, stored in a retrieval system or transmitted in any form or by any means, electronic, mechanical, photocopying, recording or otherwise without the prior permission of the publisher or in accordance with the provisions of the Copyright, Designs and Patents Act 1988 or under the terms of any license permitting limited copying issued by the Copyright Licensing Agency.

ISBN-13: 978-0-9894680-6-0

Published by:
Divine Works Publishing
Royal Palm Beach, Florida USA
www.divineworkspublishing.com
561-990-BOOK (2665)

ACKNOWLEDGEMENTS

I had asked my close friends and immediate family for help with my writing, when my life suddenly changed without notice.

I was living in Miami, caring for my mother, who had become seriously ill. I stopped writing and fell into a slight depression. A dear friend, Laura Andrews from Queens, NY, called me on the phone, she was very inspiring. Laura's encouragement felt like words straight from God's mouth to my heart.

I gave excuses of why I couldn't write and complained how most of my materials were back home in New York. Laura was not letting me off the hook. I began to listen. The following morning, I woke up and started writing poems and prayers. It seemed like my heart just opened up and the words just kept flowing.

You are never too old to fulfill your dreams! In October 2015, I met an 88 year old woman, who had written her book; Miss Daisy Marsh Ferguson was her name. We became friends and she encouraged me all the more. Ms. Daisy is a beautiful, spiritual person and I thank her very much for her kind words.

I would also like to thank Mr. Brown, an author who I met on a bus trip, who was so helpful and informative. I thank him for his valuable insight and for sharing so much of his knowledge with me.

I'd also like thank my son, Terry, who became my proofreader, without his help this book would not have been completed.

A well deserved thanks to Mr. Billy Mitchell for assisting with typing the original manuscript to this book.

A special thanks to my "Awesome Family". To all my children, grandchildren, and great children.

The Spirit of the Lord operated through these individuals, in different ways, to help me get through a rough patch in my life, and in that same spirit I pray this book helps to uplift and encourage your spirit.

THIS BOOK IS DEDICATED TO

My Gorgeous Mother

Annie Lee Farmer-Mitchell

Praise God!

TABLE OF CONTENTS
LIFESTYLE POETRY FROM THE INNER CITY

LIFE pg.11

PEOPLE pg.21

INSPIRATION pg.31

CELEBRATION pg.43

GRATITUDE pg.51

LOVE pg.59

DEDICATION pg.65

ANNE'S HAIKU'S pg.71

LIFE

? QUESTIONS ?

What makes a brother shoot a gun, killing another man's son?
What makes us want to kill? Is it some terrific thrill?
Is it jealousy? Can't have what you see?
I am you and you are me. Ain't I my Brother's Keeper?

What happened to love for each other?
What makes a brother shoot a gun, killing another man's son?
They say Black Lives Matter, is that true?
There are those who say "yeah", but still they kill each other.

"He's running, shoot him. Why?
He's Black and I fear for my life".

What happened to your priorities?
Education was a priority, education is your foundation,
without it you are lost —while others continue to be the boss.
How can we survive? When will stability kick in?

If this is so, let us all engage in stopping the violence
on each other.
What makes a brother shoot a gun, killing another man's son?
Respect for the community is missing,
No hugging and kissing.

What makes a brother shoot a gun killing another?
Now we blame it on the drugs and booze?
These new rules or just blasts from the past?

6 O'CLOCK NEWS

I listened to the news yesterday and I heard
The reporter say, "Boy shot dead".
I thought to myself "That's from around the way".
When will it stop?
A boy today, a man yesterday
And another maybe tomorrow.
Lord we have to pray.
We need you Lord today.
People are dying, mothers are crying,
Fathers are in jail. Far away.
Lord we need you today.
I listened to the news today
And I heard the reporter say "Boy shot dead."
Is that another boy from around the way?
Lord we need you today.

WHAT'S HER NAME?

She sits in that same chair in the corner every day.

What did you say?

Yeah, she sits in that chair in the corner every day.

It's like she lost all hope and just died inside.

What's her name? It doesn't matter.

Things won't change, if you call her by her name.

Life stays the same.

She sits in that same chair in the corner every day.

She has the ability to come out of that corner and see something new, taste something fresh, and feel something great .

I wish she just knew she doesn't have to sit in that same chair day after day.

The Blues

Muddy Waters and BB King played the music
and sang the songs that would tell the truth.
I remember my mother talking, singing, and
Even dancing to the Blues.

Mother sometimes had a smile on her face,
Like she was out dancing with a date.
Other times she would listen with sadness.
I always felt like this blues thing just won't go away.
Looks like it's here to stay....

Any tune you choose can be used, just pat your feet, and
up comes a beat. You can play it, sing it, or dance it.
Bebop, Hip Hop... It's all the same. Now the name's
changed. "Rap", Bad Rap, Good Rap... It's The Blues.

Listen, and see, if it fits your shoes.
The sound of the music reaches your soul.
The old brings out the new...

Muddy Waters, BB King, Bessie Smith, Ella Fitzgerald
And Sarah Vaughn knew what to do,
Sing the blues just for you ... all night long.

The songs and the music just go on, and on, and on,
The Blues...

LIFESTYLE POETRY FROM THE INNER CITY

IN THE BIG CITY

Children are crying, Fathers are dying,
Mothers are hoping and waiting.
Police are circling the city, standing tall, and looking for
anyone they can haul in the paddy wagon.
Walk soft. Its Umoja stay strong in unity...

What else could go wrong?
We have our music to carry us along.
Dance, dance, for there is magic in the spirit of rhythm.
Some will know the language of our hearts.
Umoja ... Umoja ... Umoja!!!!!!!!

The spirit of the ancestors gives us the faith we need.
Seek out knowledge. Open your mind.
Adopt the legacy our brave Kings and Queens left behind.
Teach our youth to be proud of who they are and
to stand tall, like a giant of a man.

That's life in the big city.

King Adam Powell admonished us to "Keep the faith."
Martin Luther King Jr. proclaimed "We shall overcome!"
Queen Sojourner Truth asked "Ain't I a woman?"
Queen Fanning Lou Hammer's message was
"We, as a people of the colored race,
Have a human right to take a political stand
in this land"

In the Big City of the World.

PEOPLE

DR. ADAM CLAYTON POWELL JR.

Rev. Adam Clayton Powell Jr. was a wise man.
He left us with wisdom words like
"What's in your hands?
Use what you have in your hands."

Today we ask the creator to hold us as a people
in His hands.

It's much to be said, and it's much to be done.
We need the creator's mighty hands to lift us up.
Black men troubles.
Black Lives Matter.

We need to listen and understand Dr. Adam
It's quite simple.
Just research and see
What a great man the Creator made him to be.

Hold us Dear LORD.
Hold us in your mighty hands.

ARE YOU HEARING ME?

Are you hearing me?
Life is short, Maya Angelou went home,
Soon after, Ruby Dee was gone.
Are you hearing me? Elombe Brath,
A brilliant man who touched Afrika when a crisis was at hand.

BaBa John Watusi Branch with an Afrikan heart.
Who taught us to live and love our Afrikaness and culture.
He made his transition, now he is gone.

Are you hearing me?
Life is short. What dreams do you possess?
Live'm and give'm your best,
And never, ever, settle for less…
What can happen?
It might fail, but weave your thoughts
Together with positive energy and spirituality…

Are you hearing me now?
Tupac was 25 when he died,
But his work and his impact is still alive.

Are you hearing me?
Whatever you do… Do it well…
You may have some challenges, but fight like hell,
Utilize and invigorate on your behalf, self-determination.

Life is short … and time is a thief.
Are you hearing me yet???

PRESIDENT BARACK OBAMA

Our 44th President prevailed against the forces

That never meant for him to be POTUS.

They plotted and planned to gain the upper hand,

But our Father above took charge and said,

"Take your hands off of my child!"

It was awesome!

He then won a second term.

Those who plotted against him had to learn to accept

President Obama. Our Commander in Chief.

All Praise to God be.

AFRIKAN BOY AND GIRL

Today lives a little boy and little girl

who reside in a village called Jufferee, in the city of Senegal.

Senegal is gorgeous, there are very tall trees.

Some trees have huge and very sweet mangoes,

yellow, red, and some green.

The little girl is named Nia, and her friend,

the little boy is named Kojo.

Nia and Kogo are very smart

and would love to engage in school classes,

but the school is a long distance from where they live.

The two of them have a wealth of knowledge

in planting casaba and white yams.

Playing games with rocks is lots of fun and a good experience.

On special days, like the naming of a new baby or a wedding

celebration, children from other villages come to visit.

There is dancing, drum playing, singing and a Poet emerges with

the reading of a beautiful poem.

The experience is awesome and very exciting.

One day Nia's mother said a school

near the village of Jufferee was going to open.

Kojo and Nia were discussing the importance of an education.

Nia said there will be challenges,

but Kojo said, "We can do It. We are intelligent enough,

you are 7 years old and I am 8 years old. We will do it.

This story was written and dedicated to my great granddaughter Jayda Julien.

ANN M. JONES-CHEATHAM

ANCESTORS WHO HAVE GONE HOME

Mamie L. Farmer-Kenty
BaBa John Watusi Branch
Dr. Francis Chrest Westly
J.T. Farmer
Homer Farmer
Ossie Davis
Al Fredia
Nelson Mandela
Mama Hattie
Prince
Muhammad Ali
Billy Holiday
Daisy Black
Ruby Dee
Dr. John Henri Clark
Dr. Yosef Ben-Jochannan
Maya Angelo
Erick Garner
Love Williams
General Williams
Trevon Martin

In Loving Memory

INSPIRATION

INSPIRATIONAL

God has a plan for your life. Trust him.
He gives you what you need.

The Creator of the universe
Will send you the person you need in your life
At the time you need them.

Storms happen in all our lives,
But if you hold on to God's hands
He walks you through them.

Trust God, He will bring you peace.
Don't worry or become stressed out.
Worry is a prayer without faith.

The Creator of the Universe will fight your battles,
Stay in peace with yourself, and with others.
Every day is a gift from God, give thanks.

The enemy will try and steal your joy
He will show up at your job, come into your house,
Even meet you on a Sunday morning
just to divert you from going to the House of the Lord.

Don't let the enemy take your dreams from you,
"For I know the plans I have for you declares the Lord".
Jeremiah 29:11

DON'T LET THE DEVIL STEAL YOUR JOY!

Don't let the devil steal your joy.
He will come to you in many forms.
Sometimes, he comes disguised as a friend
Who puts you down and offers no encouragement.
He will try and place fear in your mind,
blocking you from thinking anything positive.
That's his way of stopping
God's blessings that are headed your way.

Don't let the devil steal your joy.
If you are feeling sad, alone, or bored.
That's the time you have to reestablish your routine,
and ask God for a positive spirit, and a glimmer of hope.
Keep people in your life that motivate you and inspire you.
Those who make you smile and show you love.

Don't let the devil steal your joy.
When you make changes in your life
You may have to let some people go.... It's all right.
God will arrange for beautiful people who will be thrilled to be
around you and those who will enhance your life .

God Has Plans for You

God has His plans for you, so follow your dreams.
Use your talents and never say I can't.
Just do it.

Every day is a new day to learn
There is room for improvement in all our lives.

When you lack faith,
You leave yourself open to being miserable.

Stay around positive minded people.
Keep your spirits up and keep your faith in God.

Life will teach you lessons.
It's about how you approach and apply them to yourself.

Be encouraged every day by the word from our Creator,
Read something spiritual daily.

If you feel like your back is against the wall
And you can't see your way,
Just hold on and trust God,
He will guide you through.

EXAMINE SELF

Examining one's inner self can be the beginning
of living a more focused and beautiful life.

Looking deep within, although frightening at times,
helps us to see what our character defects are,
so that we can learn to make choices that help us,
rather than ones that hurt us .

Self-examination helps us to develop healthy relationships
with ourselves, our family, on the job, and
most importantly with the creator.

Through practiced self-examination
every part of your life gets better
And it happens
One day at a time.

NEVER GIVE UP

God is with you when your day lacks a spark.

God is with you when everything seems dark

God is with you when the trouble starts

in your home, on the job, or in your family.

God is with you,

His Holy Spirit will take control of your life.

God is with you, never feel defeated.

He has your back.

God is with you, don't stop praying.

God can change your life very quickly.

POEM FOR THE DAY

A beautiful yellow butterfly

flew in my door today,

as I opened it to gaze at the morning view.

It seemed to know I was still here,

and it came back again

as if to share in the amazing atmosphere.

It truly is a gorgeous day,

And It looks as though this butterfly wants to play.

Around and around it flew as if saying

"I see you and I know you see me too!"

I had a smile on my face all day!

Mother Nature puts everything in its divine place.

KUUMBA
CREATIVITY

Use your creative abilities.

Each of us has the ability to be creative.

Keep believing in yourself that you can do it

and that is how you can accomplish anything.

Don't wait too long. Just start.

Keep an open mind and listen to learn.

There are others that have ideas and experiences.

From them you can grow and discern.

Always make the decision "you" feel best about.

Never give up, You may have some delays and detours

but that's what life's about.

Get up and keep moving forward.

Again I say, never give up.

No one is perfect, keep the process going.

"Creativity, is intelligence having fun". ~Albert Einstein

TODAY

It's a beautiful day.

The rain is falling…

To give the flowers a good and healthy drink of water.

Mother earth will be feeding the trees so the leaves

Will all turn green.

The pollen is at work,

Soon the flowers will burst into full colors…

Yellow, white, and green

It's going to be an awesome scene.

SOJOURN

Stay in the middle of life's journey

The road will be narrow,

But don't turn to the right

And don't turn to the left.

There is a light at the end of the tunnel.

ANN'S 10 POSITIVE STEPS TO LIFE

1. If writing gives you joy, then write. Never be discouraged . Never let anything or anyone steal your joy.

2. Learn to look at life's challenges differently.

3. Believe in yourself. Self-determination, is a tool that can be used as your life guide.

4. Rest your heart, sit back, and relax. God is in charge.

5. Love can make you blind and make you leave all your thoughts behind. Love is sweet, love is kind, Love is one day at a time.

6. When you take life for granted, is when you become the biggest looser.

7. The game of life is easy, but we complicate it trying to change it's rules.

8. There is a saying, "if you are in a hole, don't keep digging".

9. The world is full of everything good and bad.
If you learn to listen to positive thoughts that you have...
You won't fail.

10. Don't fight battles that don't matter. Time is too precious.

CELEBRATION

ANN M. JONES-CHEATHAM

Mother's Day

Every day is Mother's Day,
But there is one day that's put aside for a big celebration
And to recognize the woman that you see
And know to be your mommy.

This is a day to reflect on the relationship you have so far,
today you can reassure your mother of your love for her,
but I still say Mother's Day is every day.

Treat her like a Queen, keep it on the right track,
on her let there be no attacks.

She is a classy lady, outstanding
and excellent for the job the she does,
whether it's walking you to school
Or simply buying you a new pair of shoes.

Mother arranged your birthday parties,
making you feel you are standing on the top of a hill.

Give her your love and time
it's an awesome day,
to make her feel like a queen in every way.

Oh yes!!!
Show your love as the days, weeks, and months move on.
You never know how long before God May call her home.
It's a time you will know she was your best friend.

Mother's Day is every day that is what I say....

CELEBRATE KWANZAA

DECEMBER 26th TO JANUARY 1st

Listen! Listen! Listen!

to the sounds, the sounds of the drums...

it's the language of the heart Kwanzaa.

Soon to start.

The spirit of love is everywhere.

Time for storytelling must be told by the young and the old.

It's the spirit of love in our soul...

drums and dance fill the atmosphere.

Kwanzaa is here! Kwanzaa is here!

The children will all gather around.

One child will light the first candle.

Black represents the people.

It is lit on the 1st day of Kwanzaa, the 26th of December.

Following is a week of celebration, ending on the 1st day of January.

Don't reject the feeling, the spirits of the drums are strong.

We can keep this joy going all night long.

The addition of colors, food, and gifts all accentuate this celebration......

so you better get Hip and pass it on to the generations.

We Practice the 7 Principles – The Nguzo Saba

(7 days of Kwanzaa) :

1. Umajo –Unity

2. Kujichagulia –Self Determination

3. Ujima –Collective Work and Responsibility

4. Ujamaa –Collective Economics

5. Nia –Purpose

6. Kuumba –Creativity

7. Imani –Faith

May the awesome sounds and beautiful sights of the Kwanzaa celebration last throughout the year.

VETERAN'S DAY: A SPECIAL THANKS

Veterans Day is here again and I have the opportunity to thank

my son, Staff Sergeant Elijah D. Cheatham, who is in the U.S.

Army. My granddaughter, Ayanna T.A. Francis, who is in the U.S.

Navy, and my son Eugene Cheatham JR., who served in the U.S.

Marine Corps. My father, Henry M. Jones served in World War 2.

I am extremely proud of them.

Thank you to all men and women serving and to those who have

served. I honor you on Veterans Day,

I honor you for your bravery.

My spirit holds overflowing love for you all.

GRATITUDE

"FATHER GOD, THANK YOU FOR THE FOOD AND DRINK THAT'S PLACED ON THIS TABLE, BEFORE US. MAY IT NOURISH OUR BODIES, SOUL, AND SPIRIT, ASHE! ASHE! ASHE! AMEN."

Today, I choose to be happy.

Today, I will not let anyone steal my joy.

Today, the peace in my heart will stay.

Today, I thank the creator for this gorgeous

and awesome Wednesday.

Today is Saturday,

a beautiful day to be ever so grateful.

Rest your heart, sit back, and relax.

God really is in charge.

Thank God for Life

Thank you God,
For having your Angels
Watch over me day and night.
Your Angels are there,
Whenever I'm in despair.
Thank You God for the Angel
That whispers in my ear,
Reminding me that you, the Creator, still cares.

THANKFUL THURSDAY

Good Morning! Today I opened my door and an awesome
yellow butterfly was flying around my flowers
she lingered around as if to say, "Have a beautiful blessed day".

This butterfly must be a girl.
She casts herself like a fashion show model,
around and around she goes, but will she stop? I don't know.

"Good morning!" I wish she would stop and stay.
She look likes a shining star coming to me on thankful Thursday.
To electrify my thoughts of gratitude,
She sure is putting a show on.
I am looking at her as she glows.

You'd have to be here, to appreciate this beautiful vision, this yellow all
over butterfly flying arou nd and over my flower bush; gorgeous pink
and white flowers, it's such an attractive sight.
It's already a Good Morning and a beautiful day!
Ashe! Ashe! Amen!

ANN M. JONES-CHEATHAM

LIFESTYLE POETRY FROM THE INNER CITY

AYANNA: A NOTE OF GRATITUDE

SATURDAY / NOVEMBER 14, 2015

Today is the ending of what has been an amazing two days

in Chicago. It is my granddaughter's Ayanna Boot Camp

graduation. She is now a sailor in the Navy. I am so very proud.

She is a fine young woman, who is making positive decisions.

Ayanna is brilliant, smart, and has been holding her

independence down. She has been given many gifts.

Any task she puts her mind to, she completes with excellence.

God has blessed me to have a wonderful family.

It was amazing sitting there on the bleachers watching the

graduation ceremony. Every sailor perfectly lined up. I recall

being at my son Elijah's Army graduation; another awesome

time in my life I remember.

Ayanna, standing there holding a flag, her shoes

shinning black, and she was cleaner than the Board of Health.

The uniform tailor made, on my face a smile was placed.

I just loved it, thank you my grandchild, Ayanna T.A. Francis.

LOVE

AGING WITH LOVE

I never thought I would see the day
When my lover would slip away.
He was gorgeous and fine
So tall and handsome with beautiful brown eyes.
I fell in love at that time, woo, what a man.
I never thought I would see the day
When my lover would slip away.
Now at his age of "95" his eyes can only see
the changes in me.
I am now age 84 and I love him more and more.
The awesome years are behind us now
And a new chapter of our life journey has opened the door
to a reality that he doesn't see any more and I can't walk.
But the amazing thing is our love keeps us strong,
As life goes on.
We sit in our chair with peace and love in the atmosphere.
Our needs are no more
Just life to enjoy.

OLD SCHOOL

Hey baby what's your name?

Why?

'Cause I'm interested, so what's your name?

It's Betty Jean.

Now you want to come on the Scene?

I've got big dreams and a lot of hope.

By the way, what's your name?

Big Joe

Why big and not just Joe?

Well I earned that name, plus I don't play around with the "okey-doke". I love to inspire someone if I can.

Anyone can achieve the best that life has to offer.

You see it's a faith base you need, do you agree?

Yeah, well what about you and me? I would love to have the pleasure of taking you to a movie or a show.

Well let me think on it Big Joe,

I might just enjoy your company!

Here is my cell number....

HOPE, PEACE, AND LOVE!

Love heals all wounds

Love will give you peace

Love gives you hope

Love can bring you the light of the universe.

DEDICATION

These Pages Are Dedicated To My Son
Sergeant Elijah D. Cheatham, Musician, Artist, and Song Writer.
This is just a sample of his work...

Sergeant Elijah D. Cheatham,

is a loving husband and an awesome Father.

He loves his family and his work is brilliant.

He serves In the UNITED STATES ARMY.

I am very proud to say you are my son.

I love you and your beautiful family.

~ Mom.

THE POWER WITHIN

Within our REACH lies every dream worth taking.

Within our POWER lies every dream worth making.

Within our SIGHT lies every vision we dream of seeing.

Within our HEARTS lies everything we ever dream of being.

Within OURSELVES lies everything we'll ever need.

– Elijah D. Cheatham
I MAKE A DIFFERENCE

Sergeant Elijah has many gifts and talents. He taught himself to play the guitar and he has written several songs. He has worked with the City of New York Parks and Programs. In 2008, Sergeant Elijah formed a company while stationed in Maryland and designed T-Shirts.

SANKOFA: LOOKING BACK

I am always trying to find ways to teach
my grandchildren about their culture.
If you don't know who you are
and where you come from,
then you will never know where you are going.
We as a people must learn the meaning of Sankofa.

HAIKU'S

ANN M. JONES-CHEATHAM

Haiku poems are a traditional form of Japanese poetry. The lines rarely rhyme. African American Haikus have been around since the early 1900. Alexander Lewis, Langston Hughes, Richard Wright and Amir Baraka have written Haikus.

Ann's Haiku's

There is and African tree planted

Three hundred years ago in Miami

The tree stands huge and very strong today

                        Music is beautiful today, yeah

                    Sitting here on the beach in Florida

                        I love the gorgeous weather

The Kwanzaa season is fun

Cultural lessons done in dance and drums

The atmosphere is colorful exciting

                    Strawberries on cake looks delicious

                      Don't eat too many you get sick

                          Only eat in fruit mix

Two birds in a tree amazingly beautiful

Making sounds like love connection

You won't believe their movements

                                          Keys to life are many

                  Which doors will you choose to open today

                              All that glitters ain't gold

Very early morning in Africa

The fishermen go to sea bringing back fish

 Fish, fish and fish

                                  Butterflies beautiful on a leaf

                              The sun is beaming so very bright

                                  Like watching in the window

We must open our hearts

Change our minds

Change our attitude and show some gratitude

ABOUT THE AUTHOR

ANN M. JONES-CHEATHAM

Ann M. Cheatham is a retired Contract Administrator for the largest Health Care Workers Union in the country; 1119 SEIU. She is a poetess and community activist, and on July 9th, 2011 she received a proclamation for her work from the honorable assemblyman Leroy Comrie. Her activist work continued with the African Poetry Theatre, Cambria Heights Civic Association 1992-1993, National Council of Negro Women from 2000-present, the Aids Center of Queens 1996-1997, and numerous other programs that help to serve those in need during the Holiday Seasons.

Ms. Cheatham is the founder of bring a Toys for Tots Kwanzaa program which began 15 years ago and still continues today. She also served as board chair of the African Poetry theatre for 6 years.

Ms. Cheatham's formal education includes an Associates Degree in Business Administration. Ms. Cheatham entered Empire State College pursing a Bachelor of Science Degree in Community &

Human Services which she graduated from in 1998.

Her life as an African-American woman who has traveled to Africa on many occasions has given her rich life experiences which drive creative and expressive writings in her works.

Ms. Cheatham is a member of St. Paul Community Baptist Church in Brooklyn, New York, and St. Paul AME Church of Miami, Florida of which she is an active member in both faith communities.

Ms. Cheatham is the loving and proud mother of eight children, and an active grandmother of thirteen grandchildren and eight great grandchildren.

One of her favorite quotes is from Maya Angelou "And Still I Rise"

www.ingramcontent.com/pod-product-compliance
Lightning Source LLC
Chambersburg PA
CBHW050606300426
44112CB00013B/2097